Let's Explore India

(Most Famous Attractions in India)

BABY PROFESSOR
EDUCATION KIDS

India is a country in South Asia. It is the seventh-largest country by area, the second-most populous country. This is where YOGA originates. Just like having a YOGA, here are the "Go to" Places in India that will lead everyone to Peace and tranquility.

Kanha National Park

It is one of the tiger reserves of India and the largest national park of Madhya Pradesh state in India. The lush sal and bamboo forests, grassy meadows and ravines of Kanha provided inspiration to Rudyard Kipling for his famous novel Jungle Book.

Kanha is known for its tigers

Palolem beach

A largely unspoiled and is inhabited by both local fishermen and by foreign tourists who live in shacks along the shore or in the main village itself.

The beach is featured as the Goan residence of Jason Bourne (Matt Damon) in the film The Bourne Supremacy (2004).

DYLAN

The Kerala backwaters

A chain of brackish lagoons and lakes lying parallel to the Arabian Sea coast (known as the Malabar Coast) of Kerala state in southern India.

House boat and backwater resort
tourism in Kollam leads the Kerala
Tourism to glory.

Virupaksha Temple

This Temple is located in Hampi about 350 km from Bangalore, in the state of Karnataka in Southern India. It is part of the Group of Monuments at Hampi, designated a UNESCO World Heritage Site.

Virupaksha temple is the oldest and the principal temple in Hampi.

Golden temple

The Harmandir Sahib, also Darbar Sahib and informally referred to as the "Golden Temple",

It is the holiest Sikh gurdwara located in the city of Amritsar, Punjab, India. It represents the distinct identity, glory and heritage of the Sikhs.

The Lotus Temple

It is a Bahá'í house of worship located in New Delhi, India. The Lotus Temple derives its name from its design.

It was designed by Iranian architect
Fariborz Sahba, who won acclaim
for the project even before the temple
was completed. It subsequently
received several awards.

Taj Mahal

It is a white marble mausoleum located on the southern bank of Yamuna River in the Indian city of Agra. It was commissioned in 1632 by the Mughal emperor Shah Jahan to house the tomb of his favorite wife of three, Mumtaz Mahal.

The Taj Mahal is regarded by many as the best example of Mughal architecture and is widely recognized as "the jewel of Muslim art in India".